FAMOUS PEOPLE GREAT EVENTS

Becoming Queen Elizabeth II

Written and Illustrated by
Gillian Clements

W
FRANKLIN WATTS

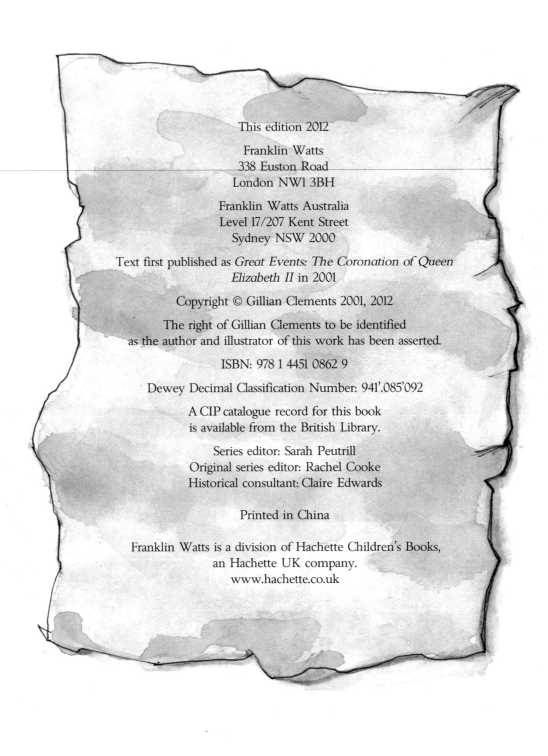

This edition 2012

Franklin Watts
338 Euston Road
London NW1 3BH

Franklin Watts Australia
Level 17/207 Kent Street
Sydney NSW 2000

Text first published as *Great Events: The Coronation of Queen
Elizabeth II* in 2001

ISBN: 978 1 4451 0862 9

Dewey Decimal Classification Number: 941'.085'092

A CIP catalogue record for this book
is available from the British Library.

Series editor: Sarah Peutrill
Original series editor: Rachel Cooke
Historical consultant: Claire Edwards

Printed in China

Franklin Watts is a division of Hachette Children's Books,
an Hachette UK company.
www.hachette.co.uk

Chapter 1

WHOOSH! BANG!
The fireworks exploded in London's skies.
Down below, thousands of excited people
pressed into Piccadilly Circus. Someone
shouted, "God Save the Queen".
Twenty-seven-year old Princess Elizabeth
had been crowned Queen that morning.
It was Tuesday, 2nd June 1953.

Britain's Prime Minister, Winston Churchill, spoke into a large BBC microphone. "We have had a day which the oldest of us are proud to have lived to see, and which the youngest will remember all their lives." The street parties continued all night.

Elizabeth was born on 21st April 1926. She was King George V's granddaughter. She called him "Grandpa England". The serious little girl and her younger sister, Margaret, lived a quiet family life, walking dogs and riding ponies.

Then in 1936, old King George V died and everything changed for young Elizabeth.

King Edward VIII, Elizabeth's Uncle, took over the throne but there was a problem. He wanted to marry Mrs Simpson, who had already been married. This was not allowed so Edward abdicated. Instead, Elizabeth's father became King George VI and her mother became Queen Elizabeth.

Chapter 2

King George VI was a quiet man who stuttered when he spoke. Being King was a terrible strain – and just three years later, the strain became far greater. Britain was at war.

German troops had invaded countries in Europe. Now, in 1940, German warplanes blitzed and bombed their way across London, killing thousands. Londoners scurried to the Underground. There were very few proper shelters.

Above, in the East End, whole streets were turned to rubble and fire. Bodies lay in their flattened homes.

Then the Germans began to bomb other British cities. Thousands of city children were evacuated – sent to live out of harm's way in the country. The princesses Elizabeth and Margaret were sent away from their London home, Buckingham Palace, too. Some nights they slept in the dungeons under Windsor Castle!

Britain had to fight back. A few hundred brave pilots fought the Germans in the skies above England. Many of them died, but they shot down even more enemy planes. The Battle of Britain saved the country from invasion.

Still the German bombing continued. The King and Queen shared their people's sorrow. When a bomb fell on Buckingham Palace the Queen wrote: "I'm glad we've been bombed. Now it makes me feel we can look the East End in the face."

On her eighteenth birthday, Princess Elizabeth joined the ATS (Auxiliary Territorial Service) as a trainee driver and mechanic. For the first time, the young princess mixed freely with people her own age. She had been educated at home, not in school with other children.

Chapter 3

At last, on the 8th May 1945, the war in Europe ended. Everyone celebrated.

"For He's a jolly good fellow," the happy crowd sang to the King outside Buckingham Palace. King George and his family stood waving from the balcony.

That night the two princesses sneaked into London's crowded streets with only a policeman and two soldiers to guard them.

"I pulled my uniform cap well down over my eyes," Elizabeth remembered.

But the street parties were soon over.
After six years of war, the British were tired.
Hundreds of thousands had been killed.
Cities were bombed out, and the country
was in debt.

"We have a great deal
of work to do to win the
peace as we won the war,"
said the new Labour Prime
Minister, Clement Attlee.

The Royal Family had
its own work to do. But the
King seemed old before his
time. Years of worry had
made him tired and ill.

Elizabeth was young –
nearly twenty. But, as heir
to the throne, she was
expected to marry. Not to
do so was "unthinkable"
said her old governess.

It's unthinkable not to marry!

So the Princess made her choice,
Prince Philip of Greece. He was a
distant cousin whom she had known
as a child. He was in the Royal Navy.

In 1947 Princess Elizabeth and
Prince Philip – now the Duke of
Edinburgh – were married
in Westminster Abbey.

It was a happy moment in a terrible year. The winter of 1947 had been the worst in living memory. There was a shortage of bread and coal, so people were hungry and cold. On top of it all, the government had to raise people's taxes to help pay the country's debts.

The King looked at the world about him. "I do wish one could see a glimmer of a bright spot in world affairs," he said. "Never in the history of mankind have things looked gloomier than they do now."

Chapter 4

Over the next few years, the King's health became worse.

Princess Elizabeth, meanwhile, had given birth to two children – Charles, born in 1948, and Anne, in 1950. Busy with her young family, she now also began to take over her father's royal duties.

In 1951 Elizabeth took the salute at Horse Guard's Parade. She looked a tiny figure as she rode to Whitehall.

In September, the King was found to have cancer, and surgeons removed a lung.

DAILY RECORD

PRINCESS TAKES KING GEORGE'S PLACE AT TROOPING OF THE COLOUR

The country was suffering too. Rationing and long queues for food continued. Everything was in short supply.

15

But some things lightened the gloom. People were cheered by Elizabeth – their fairytale princess. She and her young children gave the country hope.

In fact, things were slowly improving. The 1951 Festival of Britain had been another ray of light in dark times. Eight million people visited the festival on the south bank of the River Thames. It showed how exciting the future might be.

Now the shops began to fill with bright new things for the home. There was vinyl furniture, radiograms, washing machines, cookers and fridges. Most exciting of all was the television set!

The government was building new homes and new towns. In 1948 they had set up a National Health Service which gave free health care to everyone.

In the New Year of 1952, Elizabeth and Philip set out on a state tour to Australia, visiting Africa on the way. King George was too weak to go. He was thin and pale, as he waved goodbye to his daughter and son-in-law at London Airport.

After a few days the royal couple arrived in Kenya. They went on safari, staying at Treetops – a house nestling in the high branches of a huge old tree. They had wonderful views of the wild animals below.

Back at his royal home at Sandringham in Norfolk, King George had enjoyed a good day's shooting, but went to bed early feeling tired. That night the King died quietly in his sleep.

At dawn that day, Elizabeth and her companions had watched a huge fish eagle soar above Treetops. She didn't realise it at the time, but she was now Queen of Great Britain.

Chapter 5

It took several hours for the news of the King's death to reach the royal couple. Prince Philip broke the tragic news to his wife.

The new Queen prepared to return to England immediately.

In London the government's Cabinet met to fix a date for the Coronation. Winston Churchill was once again Prime Minister, but he was a very old man. He wanted the Queen crowned before he retired. The date was set for 2nd June 1953.

At once there was excitement in the air. Life was getting better. The country was richer and rationing was nearly at an end. "This is a new Elizabethan Age," people said. "In Elizabeth I's day, England was young and exciting. Now Queen Elizabeth II will rule a new, modern country too."

Chapter 6

People prepared for the Coronation Day
– the greatest celebration since the end of
the war. They decorated their houses and
shops in red, white and blue. Town councils
organised street parties.

Queen Elizabeth's Coronation would
be unique. TV cameras were set up at
Buckingham Palace, and inside Westminster
Abbey, where the coronation would take
place. For the first time, everyone could see
their monarch crowned! And millions around
the world could watch too.

When June arrived, crowds of people flocked to London. Thousands camped out in the Mall. In the wind and rain, they lined the route all the way from the Palace to Westminster Abbey. Twenty-five million viewers sat down to watch television. In the streets, parties began.

Just before the Queen left Buckingham Palace, news spread through the waiting crowd. People clutched at newspapers.

"On 29th May at 11.30 a.m. New Zealander Edmund Hillary and Sherpa Tensing Norgay from Nepal, reached the 29,028 feet summit of Mount Everest," they read.

It was a proud day. British and Commonwealth teamwork had made it possible for two men to stand on the roof of the world. It was the perfect news to hear on the day the Queen was crowned.

The Queen left Buckingham Palace for her Coronation in a beautiful gold coach. At the Abbey the Queen sat in St. Edward's golden throne, and the cermony began.

"Sirs, I here present unto you Queen Elizabeth, your undoubted Queen!" declared the Archbishop of Canterbury.

The Queen took her oath in a clear, high voice. She promised to rule with justice and mercy, and to protect the Church of England.

The Archbishop anointed the kneeling Queen with oil. It was time for the crowning.

The Queen sat, with symbols of state – an orb, a sceptre, the rod of mercy, and a sapphire and ruby ring. Then the Archbishop placed St. Edward's crown on to the Queen's head.

"God save the Queen!" the Lords cried.

"God save the Queen!" echoed the congregation.

The Archbishop blessed the Queen and paid homage, kissing her right hand. Then Prince Philip paid homage too. He kissed the Queen's left cheek.

The crowd was wild with excitement when they saw the newly-crowned Queen walk out of the Abbey. A cold wind lashed at the coach as it slowly returned to the Palace. Twenty-nine bands played, and thirteen thousand soldiers marched on the eleven-kilometre route.

The crowds stayed outside the Palace until nightfall. The Palace balcony was decorated in scarlet and gold. Just as the light faded, the Queen stepped out again into its floodlit glare.

"HURRAH!" The crowd cheered. They tossed streamers and hats into the air, and waved their flags.

The Queen turned on a switch, and a river of light flashed down the Mall. Soon Nelson's Column, the West End and City were bathed in light too.

Thirty thousand joyful Britons surged into Piccadilly Circus, and danced and sang until dawn.

St. Paul's

PICCADILLY

Trafalgar Square

THE STRAND

RIVER THAMES

THE MALL

Buckingham Palace

All around Britain, people were happy. They had a new, young Queen. They thought life would get better and better.

It was the dawn of a new day and a new Elizabethan Age.

Timeline

1926 26th April Elizabeth is born.

1926 General Strike in May.

1933 Adolph Hitler becomes German Chancellor.

1936 20th January George V dies and his eldest son Edward VIII becomes King.

1936 11th December Edward VIII abdicates in order to marry Wallis Simpson. They become the Duke and Duchess of Windsor.

1937 George VI is crowned.

1939 Germany invades Poland. Britain declares war on Germany. World War II begins.

1939 Women and children begin to be evacuated from London.

1940 King George VI and Queen Elizabeth visit bombed out families in London.

1940 Rationing of certain food begins.

1945 World War II ends.

1947 India gains independence from Britain marking the beginning of the end of the Empire. Princess Elizabeth marries Philip Mountbatten, then Prince of Greece.

1948 The British Labour government sets up the National Health Service.
Princess Elizabeth gives birth to her first child, Prince Charles.

1950 Princess Anne is born.

1951 The Festival of Britain.

1952 King George VI dies in February. Elizabeth becomes Queen.

1953 29th May Everest is conquered.

1953 2nd June The Coronation of Elizabeth II is watched by 25 million viewers on black and white television screens.

1954 Rationing comes to an end.

1977 Queen Elizabeth's Silver Jubilee. Peter Philips, the first of Queen Elizabeth II's grandchildren, is born to Princess Anne.

1997 Queen Elizabeth II and the Duke of Edinburgh celebrate their Golden Wedding anniversary.

2002 Queen Elizabeth's Golden Jubilee.

2007 Queen Elizabeth II and the Duke of Edinburgh celebrate their Diamond Wedding anniversary.

2012 Queen Elizabeth's Diamond Jubilee.

Quiz

Can you remember?

1. What year was Elizabeth born in?

2. What did she call George V?

3. How old was Elizabeth when she became queen?

4. Who was the Prime Minister?

5. What happened after Elizabeth's father had been king for three years?

6. Where did Elizabeth and her sister sleep when it was dangerous during the war?

7. What did Elizabeth do when she was 18?

8. Who did Elizabeth choose to marry?

9. What colours were the shops decorated for the coronation?

10. What happened on the same day that Elizabeth was crowned?

11. What are the symbols of state that Queen Elizabeth II was presented with?

12. What did people say when Queen Elizabeth II had been crowned?

Answers on page 32

Glossary

Abdicate When a King or Queen gives up their position.

Cabinet A special group of elected ministers that help govern a country.

Commonwealth The group of countries that used to be part of the British Empire and which still maintain some links. Elizabeth II is currently head of the Commonwealth.

Elizabeth I Queen of England 1558–1603.

Evacuation The movement of people from large cities to the countryside, especially during World War II.

Labour Party British political group that was formed to represent the interests of working people.

Mount Everest The highest mountain in the world, found in the Himalayas.

Rationing When the amount of food and goods you can buy is limited, or rationed, because of hard times.

The Mall The road leading from Trafalgar Square to Buckingham Palace.

Index

Quiz answers

1. 1926

2. Grandpa England

3. 27

4. Winston Churchill

5. War was declared

6. The dungeons of Windsor Castle

7. Became a trainee driver and mechanic

8. Prince Philip of Greece

9. Red, white and blue

10. The newspapers reported that Everest had been climbed

11. An orb, a sceptre, the rod of mercy and a sapphire and ruby ring

12. "God save the Queen"